I0776366

The Story of a Special Day
Volume 202

July 20

The 201st day of the year (202nd in leap years). There are 164 days remaining until the end of the year.

by Michael Dobson

Timespinner
Press

This book is also available in e-book form for Kindle, e-pub devices, and other formats from your favorite online booksellers.

For more information about the series, about us, or about your special day, please email us at editor@timespinnerpress.com.

Look for other volumes in *The Story of a Special Day,* coming often. See www.timespinnerpress.com for details and for the most recent information.

Table of Contents

Cover: Buzz Aldrin's footprint on the surface of the Moon. The Eagle landed on the lunar surface on July 20, 1969 — the COVER STORY and EVENT OF THE DAY. (Credit: NASA)

Quote of the Day

"You don't have to be a fantastic hero to do certain things — to compete. You can be just an ordinary chap, sufficiently motivated to reach challenging goals. The intense effort, the giving of everything you've got, is a very pleasant bonus."

Sir Edmund Hillary, mountaineer
born July 20, 1919

Today
in
History
THERI
ACA
MAGNA
July 20

July, by Eugène Grasset

July 20 in History

While some days of the year are more famous than others, every day of the year is filled with important, exciting, and unusual events, from religious awakenings to natural disasters, from wars to breakthroughs in technology, and from tragedy to triumph.

In this section, you'll learn about all the events that make July 20 important, including the special event that makes up our cover story or event of the day. Some events you may already know about, others may be new to you, but all of them are important parts of the history of the work. Illustrated events are shaded.

Let's explore some of the reasons why July 20 is a very special day!

Launch of Apollo 11

What Happened on July 20?

Cover Story/Event of the Day
First Manned Lunar Landing (1969)

Apollo 11, the first manned mission to the Moon, took off from Kennedy Space Center's Launch Pad 39A on July 16, 1969. Four days later, on July 20, 1969, two astronauts, Neil Armstrong and Buzz Aldrin, touched down on the lunar surface.

The Space Race between the Soviet Union and the United States effectively began with Soviet's launch of the launch of the first artificial satellite, Sputnik 1, on October 4, 1957. The US was less successful; the first Vanguard launch exploded on national television on December 6, 1957. It was not until January 1, 1958, that the US managed a successful satellite launch.

In 1959, President Dwight Eisenhower signed legislation to create the National Aeronautics and Space Administration (NASA), charged with the US space program. This transferred space efforts from the US Air Force to a new civilian agency, where the manned space flight efforts were given a new name: Project Mercury.

The Soviets continued to surge ahead. On April 12, 1961, cosmonaut Yuri Gagarin became the first human in space, completing a single orbit on April 12, 1961. Less than a month later, Alan Shepard became the first American in space, completing a suborbital flight.

These Soviet successes convinced US President John F. Kennedy of the necessity for strong leadership in the space effort, leading to his famous "We Choose to Go to the Moon" speech given in Houston on September 12, 1962.

With increased funding and support, the US launched five more missions in the Mercury program, including John Glenn's 1962 flight that completed three orbits of the Earth. The Soviets countered by launching two ships simultaneously, and on June 16, 1963, sent the first woman (and first civilian) into space, Valentina Tereshkova.

In the Gemini program, the US explored the technologies necessary to make the Moon flight, including space walks, space rendezvous, and docking. The Soviet Voskhod program pioneered three-astronaut crews and a "shirt sleeve" cabin environment, but political troubles in the Soviet Union put a long pause in their program and allowed the US to achieve parity. Ten Gemini missions gave the US a strong base of knowledge.

Both sides suffered setbacks. The first Apollo mission was destroyed when a cabin fire killed astronauts Gus Grissom, Ed White, and Roger Chaffee on the launch pad. Vladimir Komarov became the first in-flight fatality when his Soyuz 1 parachute failed on reentry.

Apollo 7 was the first Apollo mission to reach orbit, and 15 days later, the Soviets launched Soyuz 3, which attempted the first space docking. The race remained close, with both nations completing circumlunar flights in early 1969.

With both nations poised to go to the Moon, the race was increasingly tight. The Soviet N-1 rockets, however, suffered several launch failures and a major launch pad explosion. Meanwhile the US set a goal of a July 1969 lunar landing, to be achieved by Apollo 11.

The Apollo 11 crew was selected in January 1969. The Mission Commander was Neil Armstrong, the Command Module Pilot was Michael Collins, and the Lunar Module Pilot was Edwin "Buzz" Aldrin. Armstrong and Aldrin would go down to the surface of the Moon, while Collins would remain in the Command Module.

Crew of Apollo 11: From left, Neil Armstrong, Michael Collins, and Buzz Aldrin

Because the Apollo 10 crew named their spacecraft *Charlie Brown* and their lunar module *Snoopy*, the Apollo 11 crew was asked to be more serious in selecting names. They named the command module *Columbia* after Jules Verne's spacecraft in his 1865 novel *From the Earth to the Moon.* The lunar module was named *Eagle,* for the US national bird.

Millions watched the launch of Apollo 11 at 13:32:00 UTC[*] on July 16, 1969. It reached orbit twelve minutes after takeoff, and thirty minutes later fired its rockets again to head for the Moon. Once there, the spacecraft entered lunar orbit.

The *Eagle* in flight

---

[*] UTC: Coordinated Universal Time, an improved version of what was once known as "Greenwich Mean Time."

On Sunday, July 20, Armstrong and Aldrin entered the lunar module and began the descent to the Sea of Tranquility on the lunar surface. The mission nearly ended in failure when the onboard navigation and guidance computer overloaded, but the software recovered and the mission continued. Armstrong took manual control as the spacecraft neared the surface of the Moon, and at 20:17:40 UTC on July 20, they touched down on the lunar surface with only 25 seconds of fuel remaining. "Houston, Tranquility Base here," Armstrong transmitted. "The *Eagle* has landed."

"One small step"

It took several hours to get ready to set foot on the Moon, but on 02:39 UTC on Monday, July 21, 1969, Neil Armstrong opened the hatch and climbed down the ladder, with each step transmitted back to Earth with a television signal watched by million. Armstrong meant to say "That's one small step for a man, one giant leap for mankind," as he set foot on the Moon, but the "a" got lost in transmission.

The astronauts planted an American flag and uncovered a plaque on the base of the ladder: "Here men from the planet Earth first set foot upon the Moon, July 1969 A.D. We came in peace for all mankind."

The astronauts stayed on the surface for around two and a half hours, then reentered the *Eagle*. They rested for about seven hours before preparing to leave the lunar surface and rejoin *Columbia*.

Just before dawn on July 24, the *Columbia* splashed down in the Pacific Ocean and the astronauts were recovered. Although the chance of bringing back a deadly disease from the Moon was considered remote, the astronauts were quarantined for 21 days just in case.

Today, the *Columbia* can be seen at the Smithsonian's National Air and Space Museum in Washington, DC.[†]

[†] Apollo 11 command module pilot Mike Collins became director of the National Air and Space Museum during the creation of the building on the National Mall; this author was privileged to be a member of the research staff during that time.

Astronaut Buzz Aldrin

Diagram of the Pyrélophore (Photo: Daderot)

First photograph of the surface of Mars, taken by Viking 1

More July 20 Events

1807 — Nicéphor and Claude Niépce receive a patent for the **world's first internal combustion engine**, the Pyrélophore.

1848 — The **Seneca Falls Convention**, a landmark in the women's rights movement, concludes.

1917 — The Corfu Declaration establishes the Kingdom of **Yugoslavia**.

1944 — **World War II/Bomb Plot:** Adolf Hitler survives an assassination attempt led by Colonel Claus von Stauffenberg.[‡]

1968 — The first **Special Olympics** games begin in Chicago, Illinois.

1969 — The "**Football War**" between Honduras and El Salvador ends after six days.

1974 — **Cyprus Dispute:** Turkey invades the island of Cyprus. At the time of writing, it continues to occupy the northern third of the island, in spite of UN resolutions condemning it.

1976 — The **Viking 1** lander successfully touches down on the surface of Mars.

[‡] My novel (with Douglas Niles) *Fox on the Rhine* (2000) follows the Bomb Plot and its aftermath.

1977 — In response to Freedom of Information Act requests, the US **Central Intelligence Agency** reveals its program of **mind-control experiments**, known as **MKUltra**.

1997 — The restored **USS *Constitution*** ("Old Ironsides") sets sail for the first time in 116 years.

2012 — A **mass shooting** at a movie theater in **Aurora, Colorado**, kills 12 and injures 70.

2015 — The **US and Cuba restore diplomatic relations** after 44 years.

July, by George Auriol

USS *Constellation* (Photo: Journalist 2nd Cl. Todd Stevens, USN).

Quote of the Day

"There is nothing impossible to him who will try."

Alexander the Great, conqueror
born July 20, 356 BCE

17

Sir Edmund Hillary, mountaineer who led the first expedition to reach the summit of Mount Everest, born July 20, 1919

Notable July 20 People

With the current world population at about seven billion people, on average about 19 million people also celebrate their birthdays on July 20 — and that isn't counting the millions and millions who came before! No matter when you were born, you share your birthday with many special people whose accomplishments (and occasionally embarrassments) have been noted as part of history.

In this section, you'll meet fascinating people who share your birthday. They're organized by what they're famous for, and then in reverse chronological order from most recent to earliest. Those who are shown in photographs or artwork have a box around them. We don't have photos of everyone, so please forgive us if your favorite person is missing.

Some of these people you've heard of, others may be new to you, but they all make up an important part of the reason that July 20 is a truly special day!

Copy of a 3rd century BCE bust of Alexander the Great by Lysippos of Alexandria (Photo: Carole Raddato, CC BY-SA 2.0)

Who Was Born on July 20?

Person of the Day
Alexander the Great (356 BCE)

Alexander the Great, King of Macedon, was born in 356 BCE. At the age of 20, he succeeded his father Philip to the throne, and set out on an unprecedented military campaign and created one of the largest empires in the ancient world before his death at the age of 32.

Numerous legends surround the birth and early childhood of Alexander. Both parents reported prophetic dreams before he was born. On the day of Alexander's birth, his father, Philip II, learned that his generals had defeated two armies and his horses had won at the Olympic Games. The same day, the Temple of Artemis, one of the Seven Wonders of the World, burned down.

Alexander was raised as a young warrior. He tamed a horse, Bucephalas, that had refused all other riders. Bucephalas would carry Alexander through all his conquests, and when he died, Alexander named a city for him.

The young Alexander was tutored by the ancient philosopher Aristotle, and from the age of 16, accompanied his father into battle. Upon the assassination of his father, he had his rivals killed, then put down a series of revolts.

During that period, he famously encountered the philosopher Diogenes the Cynic. Alexander asked what he could do for the learned man, to which Diogenes replied that he could stand a little to the side, because Alexander was blocking the sunlight.

Alexander and Diogenes, by Sebastiano Ricci

In 334 BCE, Alexander led an army of over 54,000 troops and 120 ships crewed by 38,000 people across the Hellespont to invade the Persian Empire, then the largest and most powerful. When he took the Persian city of Gordium, he was confronted by an intricate knot. Whosoever could untangle the knot, it was said, would become king of Asia. Alexander drew his sword and cut the knot in half, the origin of the phrase "cut the Gordian knot."

Alexander cuts the Gordian knot (H. A. Guerber)

Two years later, he defeated the Persian emperor Darius in battle and forced him to flee. Alexander then conquerd Syria and made his way down the coast to Egypt, where he was proclaimed a god and founded the city of Alexandria. Turning his attention back to Persia, he took the capital city, Persepolis.

Forcing Darius to flee once again, Alexander consolidated his conquest of the Persian Empire and pushed into Central Asia, then into the lands that became modern Afghanistan and Pakistan in the Indian subcontinent.

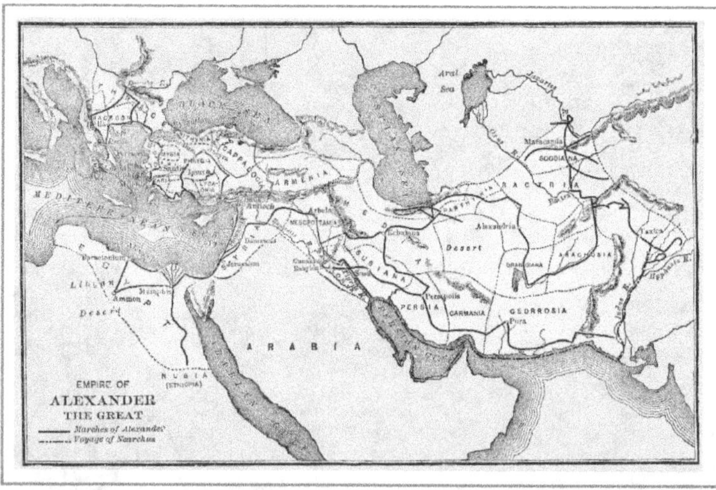

The Empire of Alexander the Great (George Willis Botsford, Ph.D.)

His soldiers had had enough by that time, and refused to go forward. Alexander returned to Persia, putting down minor rebellions and continuing to consolidate his empire.

Staying in the Babylonian palace of Nebuchad-nezzar II (famous for his Biblical conquest of the Kingdom of Judah some 200 years previously), Alexander fell ill, and died on either June 10 or 11, 323 BCE. Some claimed he had been poisoned, others have attributed his death to malaria or typhoid fever, still others to West Nile virus. His body was placed in a gold sarcophagus filled with honey, and taken back to Macedonia for entombment. His general Ptolemy seized it en route and took it to Alexandria, where it was displayed for several centuries. Julius Caesar, Pompey the Great, and Augustus all visited his tomb before it was closed to the public in 200 CE. It subsequently vanished and its fate is unknown.

Alexander's empire was divided into four parts. Ptolemaic Egypt, Seleucid Mesopotamia and Central Asia, Attalid Anatolia, and Antigonid Macedon, each ruled by one of Alexander's generals.

At its height, Alexander's empire spanned more than 2 million square miles (5.2 million square kilometers). He never lost a battle, although he was typically outnumbered by his opponents. The lands he conquered continued to trade with one another, spreading Greek influence throughout the east. Several of his cities, especially Alexandria in Egypt, have survived to the present day.

Alberto Santos-Dumont flying his aircraft *14-bis*, 1906

Alberto Santos-Dumont flying his dirigible in 1904

Other July 20 Births

Art

Judy Chicago, feminist artist best known for her 1979 work *The Dinner Party. (1939)*

Business

Mike Ilitch, founded the fast food franchise Little Caesars Pizza; owned the Detroit Red Wings and the Detroit Tigers. *(1929)*

Engineering and Technology

Alberto Santos-Dumont, Brazilian aviation pioneer in both lighter-than-air and heavier-than-air craft. He pioneered steerable lighter-than-air craft and built and flew the first manned airplane in Europe. In Brazil, he is considered to have been the first to demostrate and fly a practical airplane. *(1873)*

Exploration and Adventure

Sir Edmund Hillary, New Zealand mountaineer who, along with Nepalese Sherpa mountaineer Tenzing Norgay, was the first climber confirmed to have reached the summit of Mount Everest. *(1919)* *(Photo page 18.)*

Fashion and Modeling

Gisele Bündchen, Brazilian supermodel listed as one of the world's most powerful women by Forbes; known for her work as a Victoria's Secret Angel. *(1980)*

Gisele Bündchen (Photo: Tiago Chediak, CC BY-SA 2.0)

Government and Politics

Enrique Peña Nieto, elected President of Mexico in 2012. *(1966)*

Barbara Mikulski, US Senator and member of Congress from Maryland; longest-serving woman in the history of the US Congress. *(1936)*

Elliot Richardson, government official who famously resigned as Richard Nixon's Attorney General rather than obey the President's order to fire Watergate special prosecutor Archibald Cox, in what became known as the "Saturday Night Massacre[§]." *(1920)*

Literature and Poetry

Alistair MacLeod, award-winning Canadian novelist known for his books set in Cape Breton. *(1936)*

Cormac McCarthy, novelist known for such books as *Blood Meridian, All the Pretty Horses,* and *No Country for Old Men,* the latter adapted into an Academy Award-winning Best Picture. *(1933)*

[§] The "Saturday Night Massacre" episode is described in detail in my book *Watergate Considered as an Org Chart of Semi-Precious Stones. (See page 93.)*

Thomas Berger, novelist best known for his 1964 novel *Little Big Man,* which was made into a 1970 film starring Dustin Hoffman. *(1924)*

Erik Axel Karlfeldt, Swedish poet awarded the 1931 Nobel Prize in Literature. *(1864)*

Petrarch, Italian Renaissance poet and scholar, sometimes called the "father of Humanism." *(1304)*

Petrarch (Francesco Petrarca)

Music

Tobi Vail, founding member of Bikini Kill and coined the spelling of "grrl." *(1969)*

Kool G Rap, influential rapper who pioneered mafioso rap. *(1968)*

Kool G Rap (Photo: Kanamedia, CC BY-SA 2.5)

Courtney Taylor-Taylor, lead singer and guitarist for The Dandy Warhols. *(1967)*

Stone Gossard, rhythm and additional lead guitarist for Pearl Jam. *(1966)*

Chris Cornell, lead vocalist for Soundgarden and Audioslave. *(1964)*

Mick MacNeil, Scottish songwriter and keyboardist best known as a member of the group Simple Minds. *(1958)*

Paul Cook, drummer for the punk rock band the Sex Pistols. *(1956)*

Jay Jay French, founding member and guitarist of Twisted Sister. *(1952)*

Carlos Santana, Mexican-American musician listed by *Rolling Stone* as one of the greatest guitarists of all time; hits include "Evil Ways," "Oye Como Va," and "Black Magic Woman." *(1947)*

John Lodge, best known as bass guitarist, vocalist, and songwriter of The Moody Blues. *(1945)*

Kim Carnes, singer-songwriter best known for her 1981 Grammy Song and Record of the Year, "Bette Davis Eyes." *(1945)*

T. G. Sheppard, country singer-songwriter who had 14 number one hits on the US country charts in the 1970s and 1980s. *(1944)*

Carlos Santana (Photo: Chris Hakkens, CC BY-SA 2.0)

Buddy Knox, singer-songwriter best known for his 1957 hit "Party Doll." *(1933)*

Topps "recording star" trading card for Buddy Knox

Mort Garson, songwriter and arranger best known for his hits "Our Day Will Come" (composer) and "Guantanamera" and "By the Time I Get to Phoenix" (arranger). *(1924)*

Cindy Walker, country singer-songwriter whose best known compositions incude "You Don't Know Me," "When My Blue Moon Turns to Gold Again," and "Bubbles in My Beer." Member of the Country Music Hall of Fame. *(1918)*

Performing Arts

John Francis Daley, known for his roles on *Freaks and Geeks* and *Bones*. *(1985)*

Judy Greer, actress in films including *The Wedding Planner* and *What Woman Want,* as well as television series *Arrested Development, It's Always Sunny in Philadelphia, Californication,* and *Archer*. *(1975)*

Roberto Orci, screenwriter and producer who co-created the TV series *Fringe* and *Sleepy Hollow*. *(1973)*

Omar Epps, played Dr. Gant on *ER* and Dr. Foreman on *House*. *(1973)*

Sandra Oh, actress best known for playing Cristina on the medical drama *Grey's Anatomy,* for which she received multiple awards. *(1971)*

Josh Holloway, actor best known for playing Sawyer on the TV series *Lost*. *(1969)*

Carlos Saldanha, director and producer of animated films including *Ice Age, Rio, Robots* and others. *(1965)*

Carlos Alazraqui, comedian and voice artist known for his work on *Reno 911!, Phineas and Ferb, The Fairy OddParents,* and *Family Guy;* also voiced the Taco Bell chihuahua in numerous commercials. *(1962)*

Jeff Rawle, played George Dent in the British sitcom *Drop the Dead Donkey* and Amos Diggory in *Harry Potter and the Goblet of Fire. (1951)*

Muse Watson, actor who played the villain in the *I Know What You Did Last Summer* franchise and had regular roles in the television series *Prison Break* and *NCIS. (1948)*

Wendy Richard, best known for her long-time roles on the television series *Are You Being Served?* and *EastEnders. (1943)*

Natalie Wood, actress who became a star at age 8 in 1947's *Miracle on 34th Street;* other major films include *Rebel Without a Cause, West Side Story, Gypsy, Splendor in the Grass,* and *Love With the Proper Stranger.* Received four Academy Award nominations for Best Actress and Best Supporting Actress. *(1938)*

Diana Rigg, English actress best known for playing Emma Peel in the 1960s television series *The Avengers,* Olenna Tyrell in the 2010s series *Game of Thrones,* as well as numerous films; hosted the PBS series *Mystery!* for 14 years; received a knighthood in 1994. *(1938)*

Natalie Wood

Sally Ann Howes, actress and singer best known for playing Truly Scrumptious in the 1968 film *Chitty Chitty Bang Bang. (1930)*

Heather Chasen, English actress best known for soap opera roles on such shows as *Crossroads* and *EastEnders. (1927)*

Lola Albright, best known as co-star of the television series *Peter Gunn*; films include *Kid Galahad* (with Elvis Presley) and *The Tender Trap* (with Frank Sinatra). *(1924)*

Verna Felton, voice actress known for roles in numerous Disney films, including the Fairy Godmother in *Cinderella*, as well as roles in *Dumbo, Alice in Wonderland, Lady and the Tramp, Sleeping Beauty,* and *The Jungle Book*, along with voicing Fred's mother in Hanna-Barbera's *The Flintstones. (1890)*

Religion and Philosophy

Dobri Dobrev (Добри Добрев), known as the "Saint of Bailovo," Bulgarian ascetic who walked over 20 kilometers a day to stand in front of a cathedral in Sofia to collect money for charity, even after he turned 100 years of age. *(1914)*

Dobri Dobrev (age 94) in front of the Alexander Nevski Cathedral, Sofia, Bulgaria. (Photo: Nexus Infinitus, CC BY-SA 4.0)

Anne Hutchinson, Puritan religious figure and leader of the Antinomian, or Free Grace, movement that challenged dominant Puritan ideas concerning religious works and behavior. She and her supporters were tried for heresy, excommunicated, and banished, settling in what became Rhode Island. She is an ancestor of US President Franklin D. Roosevelt and both Presidents Bush. *(1591**)*

Science and Medicine

Gerd Binnig, won the 1986 Nobel Prize in Physics for inventing the scanning tunneling microscope. *(1947)*

Tadeusz Reichstein, Polish-Swiss chemist who received the 1950 Nobel Prize in Physiology or Medicine for his work leading to the discovery of cortisone; developed the Reichstein process still used for the artificial synthesis of Vitamin C. *(1897)*

Ruggero Oddi, Italian physiologist and namesake of the Sphincter of Oddi, located at the end of the bile and pancreatic ducts. Inflammation of that region is known as "odditis." *(1864)*

Sir Richard Owen, biologist and paleontologist best remembered for coining the word *Dinosauria* ("fearfully great reptile"), which became our modern word "dinosaur." *(1804)*

** Baptismal date. At that time, baptismal dates were more important than birth dates in some communities. The actual date of Anne Hutchinson's birth is unknown.

Sports

Charles Johnson, MLB catcher who won four consecutive Gold Glove Awards; one of only three catchers to catch at least 100 games in a single season without committing an error. *(1971)*

Mel Daniels, basketball player for the New York Nets and for various ABA teams; member of the Naismith Memorial Basketball Hall of Fame. *(1944)*

Mel Daniels

Tony Oliva, right fielder and designated hitter who played 15 yars for the Minnesota twins, named 1964 American League Rookie of the Year. *(1938)*

Chuck Daly, led the Detroit Pistons to two consecutive NBA championships and coached the "Dream Team" 1992 US men's Olympic basketball team" to win the gold medal. Two-time inductee into the Naismith Memorial Basketball Hall of Fame. *(1930)*

Heinie Manush, outfielder and coach in major league baseball for more than 20 years, member of the Baseball Hall of Fame. *(1901)*

1933 Goudey baseball card of Heinie Manush

July, by Joachim von Sandrart

Pancho Villa (Photo: George Grantham Bain)

Who Died on July 20?

Government and Military

Vince Foster, deputy White House counsel in the beginning of President Bill Clinton's administration; his suicide led to numerous conspiracy theories. *(1983)*

Joseph Rochefort, US Navy cryptanalyst who helped break the Japanese JN-25 code during World War II, and uncovered the date and location of the impending Japanese attack on Midway allowing the US Navy to respond in time. *(1976)*

Ludwig Beck, German general and Army chief of staff in the early years of the Nazi regime; later opposed to Hitler; killed for his involvement in the Bomb Plot *(see page 13). (1944)*

Felix Dzerzhinsky (Фе́ликс Дзержи́нский), Bolshevik leader best known for establishing the first Soviet secret police force, known as Cheka (ЧК). *(1926)*

Pancho Villa, Mexican revolutionary general and government leader, hunted by the US government in the Pancho Villa Expedition led by General John J. Pershing. *(1923)*

Journalism

Helen Thomas, UPI and later Hearst reporter who served as White House correspondent and bureau manager during ten Presidential administrations. *(2013)*

Helen Thomas (Photo: *US News and World Report*)

Frank Reynolds, television journalist and anchorman of the *ABC Evening News, World News Tonight,* and *Nightline. (1983)*

Literature and Poetry

Jan Struther, English writer best known for novels and stories featuring her character *Mrs. Miniver,* made into a 1942 film. *(1953)*

Paul Valéry, influential French poet and philosopher, nominated twelve times for the Nobel Prize in Literature. *(1945)*

Music

Chester Bennington, lead singer for Linkin Park and Stone Temple Pilots. *(2017)*

Wayne Carson, country music artist whose fmous famous songs are "Neon Rainbow," "The Letter," and "Always on My Mind." *(2015)*

Performing Arts

Theodore Bikel, stage actor who created the role of Captain von Trapp in *The Sound of Music,* and the long-running Broadway hit *Fiddler on the Roof. (2015)*

James Doohan, actor best known for playing Scotty the engineer in the *Star Trek* franchise; wounded in the D-Day invasion of Normandy. *(2005)*

James Doohan as Scotty on *Star Trek*

Sandra Gould, actress best known for playing Gladys Kravitz on the sitcom *Bewitched. (1999)*

Richard Egan, actor in numerous films and television series, including *Love Me Tender* (with Elvis Presley) and *Empire. (1987)*

Bruce Lee, actor, filmmaker, and martial artist who appeared in the television series *The Green Hornet* and in iconic roles in such films as *Fists of Fury* and *Enter the Dragon*; developed the martial art Jeet Kune Do. *(1973)*

Bruce Lee in *Fists of Fury*

Pioneers

Peregrine White, first known English child born to the Pilgrims in America. *(1704)*

Religion

Tammy Faye Bakker, televangelist and co-host of The PTL Club with her husband Jim Bakker, who was implicated in a scandal involving rape and financial irregularities; often mocked for her heavy use of makeup. *(2007)*

Science and Mathematics

Guglielmo Marconi, Italian inventor and engineer credited as the inventor of radio; shared the 1909 Nobel Prize in Physics for his work in wireless telegraphy. *(1937)*

Andrey Markov (Андрéй Мáрков), mathematician best known for his work on stochastic processes; developed Markov chains and numerous theorems. *(1922)*

Bernhard Riemann, pioneering mathematician known for the Riemann integral, analytic number theory, and differential geometry, laying the foundation of the mathematics of general relativity. *(1866)*

Guglielmo Marconi in front of his early radio apparatus

Quote of the Day

"Balance your thoughts with action. — If you spend too much time thinking about a thing, you'll never get it done."

Bruce Lee, martial artist and actor
died July 20, 1973

Holidays Around the World
July 20

"Four Hands Holding," by Vicki Nunn — for **Día del Amigo**, or **Friendship Day**

July 20 Holidays and Celebrations

If you're looking for a reason to take your special day off, you should know that every single day is a holiday somewhere in the world! Here's some of what you can celebrate on July 20!

General Events

Declaracion de la Independencia de Colombia (Colombia)

The nation of Colombia celebrates this day for its declaration of independence from Spain, which took place July 20, 1810.

Día del Amigo (Argentina, Brazil)

Many nations set aside a day to honor friendship. While International Friendship Day is observed on July 30, the South American nations of Argentina and Brazil celebrate Friendship Day on July 20.

Día del Ingeniero (Costa Rica)

Engineer's Day in Costa Rica marks the July 20, 1949 foundation of the Pan American Union of Engineering Association.

Día del Lempira (Honduras)

Lempira's Day in Honduras commemorates the warrior leader of the Lenca tribe who led the (unsuccessful) resistance to the Spanish conquest of the region in the 1530s. Lempira is a folk hero to the Honduran people. The Honduran currency is named the Lempira in his honor.

International Chess Day (worldwide)

The world of chess celebrates International Chess Day on the anniversary of the July 20, 1924, founding of the International Chess Federation (FIDE). Chess events and tournaments take place in over 150 countries each year.

"The Chess Players," by Honoré Daumier — for **International Chess Day**

National Tree Planting Day (Central African Republic)

Many nations celebrate an Arbor Day or Tree-Planting Day. In the Central African Republic, National Tree Planting Day is observed each July 20.

Space Exploration Day/Moon Day (worldwide)

The exploration of space is celebrated on the anniversary of the first manned landing on the Moon. *(See page 5.)*

Religious Feast Days and Holidays

Saint Days

Each day in the year is considered a feast day for one or more saints. They are somewhat different in western Christianity (Catholicism and many forms of Protestantism) and in eastern (Orthodox) Christianity.

In *Western Christianity*, July 20 is the feast day of the prophet Elijah and Saints Ansegisus, Apollinaris of Ravenna, Aurelius, Ealhswith,, John Baptist Yi, Margaret the Virgin, Thorlac, and Wilgefortis. The Episcopal Church USA also honors abolitionists and women's rights advocates Elizabeth Cady Stanton, Amelia Bloomer, Sojourner Truth, and Harriet Ross Tubman.

In *Eastern Orthodox Christianity*, it is also the commemoration of Saints Elias of Jerusalem, Flavius of Antioch, and Abramius of Galich. (These saints are honored on August 2 by "Old Calendrists.[tt]")

[tt] "Old Calendrists" use the older Julian calendar rather than the modern Gregorian calendar for liturgical purposes. For more about the different types of calendars, see "What Day of the Week is July 20?"

Celebrations About Food

In the United States, almost every day of the year is dedicated to a particular food — some days honor more than one!. Sponsored by manufacturers, retailers, farmers, or simply fans, these days are often proclaimed by the President, Congress, state governors, or mayors.

In the US, July 20 is all about sweets. It's **National Ice Cream Sundae Day, National Lollipop Day, International Cake Day,** and **Fortune Cookie Day,** all at the same time! If July 20 happens to fall on the third Sunday, it's also **National Ice Cream Day** (sundae optional).

The entire month of July is dedicated to the following foods.

- National Baked Beans Month
- National Blueberry Month
- National Candy Month
- National Culinary Arts Month
- National Fruit and Veggies Month
- National Grilling Month
- National Honey Month
- National Hot Dog Month
- National Ice Cream Month
- National Pickle Month
- National Picnic Month
- National Rosé Wine Month
- National Watermelon Month

People eating hot dogs, from the 1914 film *Josie's Coney Island Nightmare* — for **National Hot Dog Month**

The New York Marble Bar and Ice Cream Parlor, 1912 — for
**National Ice Cream Day, National Ice Cream Sundae Day, and
National Ice Cream Month**

A young girl talking with her Marine Corps father returning from Iraq (Credit: Sgt. Randall A. Clinton, USMC) — for **National Black Family Month** and **Cell Phone Courtesy Month**

Honorary Months

Presidents, Congresses, and nations around the world issue proclamations recognizing particular months to honor certain causes. These events generally fall in July, though honorary months do come and go.

Health

- Bereaved Parents Awareness Month
- Fragile X Awareness Month
- Group B Strep Awareness Month (US, UK)
- Herbal/Prescription Interaction Awareness Month
- Juvenile Arthritis Awareness Month
- National Wheelchair Beautification Month

Recreation

- Family Golf Month
- National Park and Recreation Month
- National Vacation Rental Month
- Women's Motorcycle Month

Society

- Cell Phone Courtesy Month
- Get Ready for Kindergarten Month
- National Black Family Month

Moveable Events

Some celebrations shift their dates from year to year, occurring on the "first Thursday" or "fourth weekend." Here are some moveable events that sometimes occur on or include July 20.

Gregorian Calendar
- Captive Nations Week *(third week)*
- National Zookeeper Week *(third week)*
- Queen's Official Birthday (Norfolk Island) *(Monday after the second Saturday)*

Beginning of the Hindu month of Mithuna (mid-June)
- *Raja Parba* (ରଜ ପର୍ବ), three-day festival to mark the beginning of the agricultural year in the Indian state of Odisha *(Varies between March and July)*
- *Phi Ta Khon*, also known as the Ghost Festival, is a three-day Buddhist celebration in Loei province, Thailand. The date is selected annually by each town's spirit mediums.

Just for Fun

Anybody can make up a holiday, and many people do! While none of these are officially recognized and some may come and go, here are a few more holidays for July 20.

- International Surfing Day *(third Saturday)*
- Global Hug Your Kid Day *(third Monday)*
- National Get Out of the Doghouse Day *(third Monday)*

- National Flip Flop Day *(third Friday)*, United States
- World Jump Day (an annual event in which millions of people in the Western Hemisphere are supposed to jump simultaneously and move the Earth to a different orbit. Originally a hoax, it's still observed each year on July 20.

A 1911 surfer girl, by J. A. Cahill — for **International Surfing Day**

Quote of the Day

"The English winter — ending in July,
To recommence in August."

— Lord Byron, *Don Juan"*

About
the
Month
of
July

July, from the *Brevarium Grimani* by Gerard Horenbout and Simon Bening (c.1510)

July: The Seventh Month

"Hot July brings cooling showers,
Apricots and gillyflowers."
— *Sara Coleridge, "The Months".*

In the original Roman calendar, the month of July was named *Quintilis*, the fifth month, because the Romans originally counted the first of March as the beginning of the new year.

Quintilis was renamed July by the Roman senate in honor of Gaius Julius Caesar after his death in 44 BCE, because Caesar, among his other accomplishments, had undertaken a major calendar reform, known as the Julian calendar, which remained the standard European calendar until 1582 CE. (Not to be outdone, Emperor Augustus arranged for the next month, Sextilis, to be renamed in his honor.)

July is one of the seven months with 31 days. In a common (non-leap) year, it always starts on the same day of the week as April, and on the same day of the week as January in leap years. Strangely, in common years, no other month of the year ends on the same day of the week as July! (In leap years, the last day of July and January fall on the same day.)

July in Other Cultures

In Latin, the month of July was spelled *Iulius*, as the Romans did not have the letter "J."

In Albanian, the month is *korrik*. Arabs call the month يوليه *(yūlia)*.

It is юли *(juli)* in Bulgaria, *lipanj* in Croatia, and *červen* in Czech.

The Finns call the month *kesäkuu* and the Greeks call it Ιούλιος *(Ioúlios)*.

The Hebrew calendar has different months, but when they refer to the Gregorian month, it's יולי *(yûlî)*.

In Gaelic, July is *Meitheamh mi an Mheitheamh*, and in Russian, it is июнь *(ijun')*.

The Chinese use 六月 *(liùyuè* in Mandarin); Koreans 유월 *(yuweol)*; and it's 腩秪 *(tháng sáu)* in Vietnamese.

July Sayings and Superstitions

Farming

- The corn harvest will be good if the corn growing in the fields is "knee high by the Fourth of July."
- "If the first of July be rainy weather, 'twill rain more or less for four weeks together."
- "Rain or dry, plant your turnips on the Fourth of July."

- A swarm of bees in May is worth a load of hay. A swarm of bees in June is worth a silver spoon. A swarm of bees in July is not worth a fly.

Marriage

- "Those who in July do wed, must labor for their daily bread."

As for which day of the week, that's easy.

Monday for health, Tuesday for wealth,
Wednesday best of all, Thursday for losses,
Friday for crosses, Saturday for no luck at all.

 Michael Dobson

July Symbols

Birthstone: Ruby (symbolizes success, devotion, and integrity.)

According to an old English proverb, "The glowing Ruby should adorn/Those who in warm July are born,/Then will they be exempt and free/From love's doubt and anxiety."

Ruby

Birth Flowers: Water Lily (purity of heart) or Larkspur (lightness and levity.)

Water Lily (Photo: Dinkum)

Birth Tree: Elm (strength of will and intuition)

"Study of an Elm Tree," John Constable (1821)

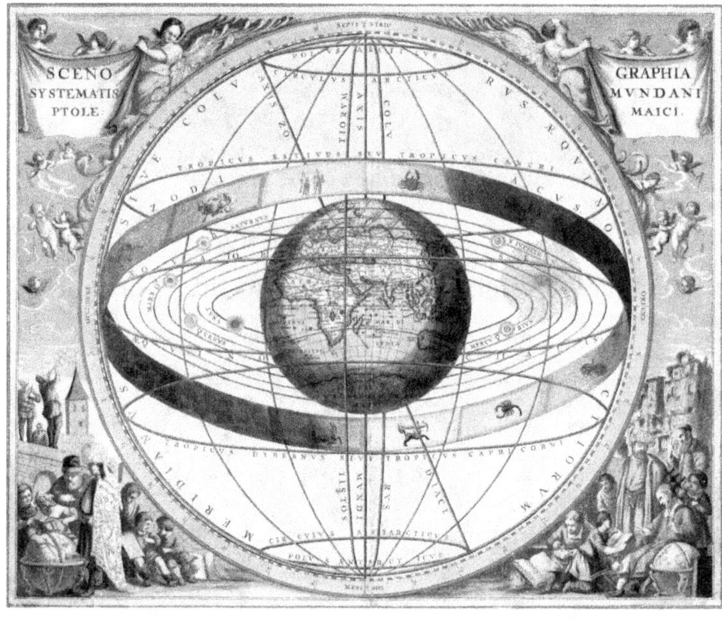

Scenography of the Ptolemaic Cosmography, by Johannes van Loon, based on Andreas Cellarius's *Harmonia Macrocosmica*, 1660

July 20 Zodiac Signs

From the perspective of someone on Earth, the Sun appears to move through the sky throughout the year, along a path astronomers call the *ecliptic plane*. The ecliptic plane is divided into twelve constellations, known as the zodiac, based on traditionally observed patterns of stars. On your birthday, you can't see your constellation, because it's in the daytime sky.

The zodiac was first developed by Babylonian astronomers about 2,500 years ago. Because they were unaware that the Earth wobbles like a spinning top (known as *precession*), they didn't make allowance for the fact that the Sun's path through the zodiac changes over time.

That means there are now two sets of dates for your birth sign. The *tropical dates* are the original Babylonian dates; the *sidereal dates* tell you where the Sun actually appears as it moves along its annual path.

July 20, however, is one of the few days each year in which the tropical and sidereal sign is the same: **Cancer.**

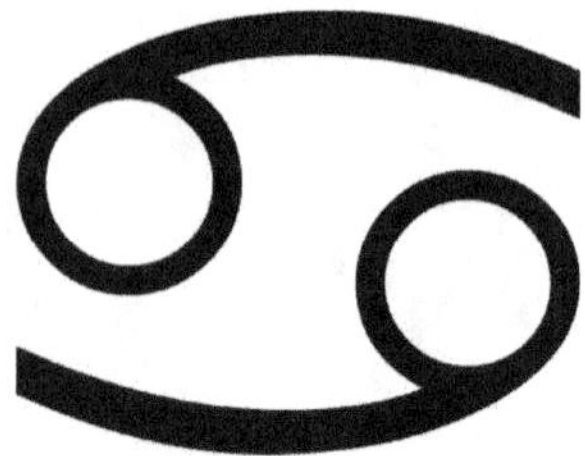

Cancer

Tropical June 21 to July 22
Sidereal July 16 to August 15

The Greek word for "crab" is Καρκινος (Karkinos), later Latinized as carcinus, which evolved into our word cancer. In Greek mythology. In one telling, when Hercules was battling the Hydra, Zeus's wife Hera sent Karkinos to distract the hero, but Hercules kicked it with such force that it was thrown into the sky, becoming a constellation. (Some say that Hercules crushed the crab with his foot and that Hera placed the crab in the night sky as a reward for its service.)

Because of the association with the disease, some astrologers refer to those born under the sign of Cancer as "moon children," because the ruling planet of Cancer is the Moon.

Cancers (or Moon Children) are supposed to be loyal, dependable, caring, and adaptable, but can also be moody, self-pitying, and oversensitive. Cancers are supposed to be particularly compatible with Scorpios, Piceans, and other Cancers.

The Sign of Cancer, by Giovanni Maria Falconetto (Courtesy Palazzo d'Arco, Mantua, Italy)

Illustration by Edward Penfield

What Day of the Week is July 20?

On what day of the week does July 20 fall?

Surprisingly, this isn't an easy question. Because the calendar year is 365 days long (366 in leap years), it doesn't divide evenly by the seven days of the week.

Also, the Earth goes around the Sun in about 365-1/4 days, so a calendar tends to drift over time. That's why the same date falls on different weekdays in different years.

This is made even more complicated by a change in calendars that took place in 1582. Our modern calendar has its roots in ancient Rome, in a calendar reform conducted by Julius Caesar. Caesar commissioned mathematicians to attack the problem, and they came up with the idea of leap years, and thus standardized the calendar for centuries to come. This was called the Julian calendar.

Over time, however, the small errors in Caesar's calculation compounded. That's why Pope Gregory XIII commissioned the Gregorian calendar, used in most of the world today. Some countries converted in 1582, when the calendar was first developed; some converted later; other still haven't changed.

Gregorian and Julian aren't the only types of calendars. The Hebrew year, the Islamic year, and many other calendars are used in different parts of the world and among different people.

You can convert Gregorian dates to other calendars, including the Hebrew calendar, the Islamic calendar, and even the Mayan calendar by visiting the Fourmilab Calendar Converter at http://www.fourmilab.ch/documents/calendar/.

Chinese calendar systems are quite complex and have changed several times; a full discussion is far beyond the scope of this book. If you're interested, you can find information here: http://www.hermetic.ch/cal_stud/chinese_cal.htm.

On Names and Dates

Historians use "CE" (Common Era) and "BCE" (Before the Common Era) instead of the more common "AD" (Anno Domini, or Year of Our Lord) and "BC" (Before Christ), reflecting the fact that the year-numbering system established by the Gregorian calendar is used throughout the world in many countries not culturally Christian.

The CE/BCE designation dates back to at least 1708, and has been adopted as a standard by the United Nations and the Universal Postal Union. Because this series of books covers events and people of all nations and cultures, we use the CE/BCE terms.

The abbreviation "O.S." ("Old Style") and "N.S." ("New Style") on some dates refers to the fact that the Russian Empire (in particular) did not switch from the Julian to the Gregorian calendar at the same time as the rest of Europe, and therefore some figures and events have two dates.

Also, in the Julian calendar in England in the 16th century, the year began on March 25 rather than January 1. To avoid confusion with Gregorian dates, dates between January and March were often written using both years.

People and events whose original names are not in the Western alphabet have their native names (where possible) in the appropriate script shown in parenthesis. If you are using an e-reader to access an electronic version of this book, all characters don't always display on all devices.

A 50-year brass perpetual calendar.

Quote of the Day

"Time is an illusion, lunchtime doubly so."

Douglas Adams,
from *The Hitchhiker's Guide to the Galaxy*

Notes
and
Credits
THER
ACC
MAGNA
Timespinner
Press

Cartoon by John T. McCutcheon

Copyright, Credit, and Contact

Follow Us

Our blog "This Day in History" (http://
timespinnerpress.com/this-day-in-history/) features short
articles on events and people associated with each day, and
updates several times each week. Also subscribe to the
"Quote of the Day" at http://timespinnerpress.com/quote-
of-the-day/. You can get daily links by following us on
Facebook at TimespinnerPress, or on Twitter as
@sidewisethinker.

Contact Us

Find an error or a format problem? Want information about
the series, about us, or about when the volume for your
special day might be available? Please email us at
editor@timespinnerpress.com. (We also take requests if your
special day isn't yet complete. Please give us at least six
weeks' notice if possible.)

Sources

We owe a great debt to Wikipedia, which is our first stop for
research. We attempt to make independent confirmation of
all important dates and facts through a variety of other
sources.

Other sources we frequently use include the Library of
Congress; "on this day" listings from *Encyclopedia Britannica*,
the *New York Times*, and the BBC; Omniglot for the names of
months in other languages; *Chase's Calendar of Events*; and, of
course, the always essential Google.

All art and photographs are either in the public domain, used under a Creative Commons license, or with a "fair use" justification, and most frequently come from Wikimedia Commons and the Library of Congress Prints and Photographs Division.

Attribution is provided where possible, or as requested by the copyright owner, or when there is particular historical significance, listed below. For information about any particular illustration or photograph, please contact us.

Credits

1. The cover photograph of Buzz Aldrin's footprint on the surface of the moon was taken July 21, 1969. It is in the public domain as a work solely created by NASA.
2. The illustration of the month of July used on the back cover is from the French Gothic illuminated manuscript *Les Très Riches Heures du duc de Berry* by the Limbourg Brothers, Jean Colombe, and an intermediate painter whose name is lost to history. It is in the public domain because its copyright has expired.
3. The box graphic used on the first page is from a 1916 pamphlet entitled "Divorce versus Democracy" authored by G. K. Chesterton, originally published in London by the Society of St. Peter and St. Paul. It is in the public domain in the US because it was published prior to 1923, and is in the public domain in all countries (including the country of origin) in which the copyright time is the author's life plus 70 years or less.
4. The graphic design for the section pages in this book is from a design originally created for a pharmacy label. It is courtesy of Wellcome Images (ICV No 11073, photo V0010813), and is used here under CC BY-SA 4.0.
5. The 1896 illustration *July* by Eugène Grasset is in the public domain because its copyright has expired. The photograph of the liftoff of Apollo 11 is in the public domain as a work created solely by NASA.

6.   The photograph of the crew of Apollo 11 is in the public domain as a work created solely by NASA.

7.   The photograph of the Apollo 11 lunar module is in the public domain as a work created solely by NASA.

8.   The photograph of the first step on the Moon is in the public domain as a work created solely by NASA.

9.   The photograph of the plaque of Apollo 11 is in the public domain as a work created solely by NASA.

10. The photograph of Buzz Aldrin on the Moon is in the public domain as a work created solely by NASA.

11. The photograph of the Pyrélophore was taken by Daderot in 2011, who released the image into the public domain.

12. The photograph of the surface of Mars taken by Viking 1 is in the public domain as a work created solely by NASA.

13. The 1912 illustration of the month of July by George Auriol is in the public domain because its copyright has expired.

14. The 1997 photograph of the USS *Constellation* was taken by Journalist 2nd Class Todd Stevens, and was released by the US Navy with ID 970721-N-013S-001. It is in the public domain as a work created by a sailor in the US Navy as part of that person's official duties.

15. The 1953 photograph of Edmund Hillary was taken by an unidentified person, and was donated to the Alexander Turnbull Library in Wellington, New Zealand. It is in the public domain in its country of origin because it was taken or published prior to January 1, 1967, and the creator is anonymous.

16. The 2013 photograph of a marble copy of a bust of Alexander the Great by Lysippos of Alexandria was taken by Carole Raddato, and is used here under CC BY-SA 2.0.

17. The painting *Alexander and Diogenes* by Sebastiano Ricci was created circa 1700, and is in the public domain because its copyright has expired.

18. The 1896 illustration of Alexander cutting the Gordian knot appeared in H. A. Guerber's book *The Story of Greeks*. It is in the public domain because its copyright has expired.

19. The 1913 map of Alexander the Great's empire first appeared in George Willis Botsford's book *A History of the Ancient*

World (London: MacMillan). It is in the public domain because its copyright has expired.

20. The 1906 newspaper photograph of Alberto Santos-Dumont in *14-bis* is in the public domain because its copyright has expired.

21. The 1904 photograph of Alberto Santos-Dumont flying his airship is in the public domain because its copyright has expired.

22. The photograph of Gisele Bündchen at the Fashion Rio Verão 2007 is by Tiago Chediak, and is used here under CC BY-SA 2.0.

23. The portrait of Francesco Petrarca (Petrarch) is by an unknown artist sometime in the 14th century. It is in the public domain because its copyright has expired.

24. The 2006 photograph of Kool G Rap was taken by Kanamedia, and is used here under CC BY-SA 2.5. The image has been cropped.

25. The 1978 photograph of Carlos Santana was taken by Chris Hakkens, and is used here under CC BY-SA 2.0.

26. The 1957 Topps trading card of Buddy Knox is in the public domain because it was published in the United States between 1923 and 1963, and although there may or may not have been a copyright notice, the copyright was not renewed.

27. The 1964 publicity photo of Natalie Wood is in the public domain because it was first published in the United States between 1923 and 1977 without a copyright notice. Typically, publicity photographs are not copyrighted because of the way in which they are intended to be used.

28. The 2006 photograph of Dobri Dobraz was taken by Nexus Infinitus, and is used here under CC BY-SA 4.0.

29. The 1967 photo of Mel Daniels is in the public domain because it was first published in the United States between 1923 and 1977 without a copyright notice.

30. The painting *July* by Joachim von Sandrart was created in 1642, and is in the public domain because its copyright has expired. It is in the collection of the Staatsgalerie im Neuen Schloss, Schleißheim, Germany.

31. The photograph of Pancho Villa was taken by George
     Grantham Bain between 1910 and 1915. It is part of the
     George Grantham Bain Collection donated to the Library of
     Congress (LC-B2-2203-10). It is in the public domain because
     its copyright has expired. The image has been cropped.

32. The 1976 photograph of Helen Thomas is cropped from a
     larger image with President Gerald Ford. It was taken by a
     staff photographer of *US News and World Report*, and is part
     of the *US News and World Report* collection donated to the
     Library of Congress (digital ID ppmsca.08533). In the deed
     of gift, *US News and World Report* entered the collection into
     the public domain.

33. The publicity photo of James Doohan from *Star Trek* was
     taken between 1966 to 1969. It is in the public domain
     because it was first published in the United States between
     1923 and 1977 without a copyright notice.

34. The 1973 publicity photo of Bruce Lee in *Fists of Fury* is in
     the public domain because it was first published in the
     United States between 1923 and 1977 without a copyright
     notice.

35. The pre-1937 photograph of Guglielmo Marconi and his
     early radio apparatus was taken by an unidentified
     photographer. It is in the collection of the Smithsonian
     Institution (SIL-14-M001-13), and according to the
     Smithsonian, there are no known copyright restrictions on
     this work.

36. The 2010 photo "Four Hands Holding," was released into
     the public domain by its author, Vicki Nunn.

37. The 1863 painting "The Chess Players," by Honoré Daumier,
     is in the public domain because its copyright has expired.
     The original can be seen in the Petit Palais, Paris.

38. The 1914 photograph from the film *Josie's Coney Island
     Nightmare* is from the Billy Rose Theatre Collection, New
     York Public Library, digital ID TH-2471. It is in the public
     domain because its copyright has expired.

39. The 1912 photograph of the New York Marble Bar and Ice
     Cream Parlor, Brisbane, Australia, is from the collection of
     the State Library of Queensland (accession number 6841). It
     is in the public domain according to its uploader because its
     copyright has expired.

40. The 2009 photograph of a girl talking with her father was taken by Sgt. Randall A. Clinton, USMC, and was released by the Marine Corps with the ID 091125-M-4003C-034. It is in the public domain as a work created by an employee of the US government as part of that person's official duties.

41. The July 1911 cover of *Sunset* magazine, illustrated by J. A. Cahill, is in the public domain because its first publication occurred prior to January 1, 1923.

42. The painting "July" is from the *Brevarium Grimani*, by Gerard Horenbout and Simon Bening, and was created circa 1510. It is in the public domain because its copyright has expired.

43. The photograph of a ruby was released into the public domain by its creator.

44. The photograph of a water lily at Kew Gardens was taken by "Dinkum," who released it into the public domain under the CC0 1.0 dedication.

45. The 1821 painting "Study of an Elm Tree" by John Constable is in the public domain because its copyright has expired. The painting is in the collection of the Victoria & Albert Museum, London.

46. The celestial sphere is from *Scenography of the Ptolemaic Cosmography*, by Johannes van Loon, based on Andreas Cellarius's *Harmonia Macrocosmica*, 1660. It is in the public domain because its copyright has expired.

47. The fresco "Sign of Cancer" by Giovanni Maria Falconetto was painted between 1515 and 1520, and is in the public domain because its copyright has expired. The image is courtesy Palazzo d'Arco, Mantua, Italy.

48. The 1906 automobile calendar is by Edward Penfield, and is in the collection of the Library of Congress Prints and Photographs Division. It is in the public domain because its copyright has expired.

49. The 50-year perpetual calendar photograph is in the public domain.

50. The cartoon by John T. McCutcheon is from his 1905 collection *The Mysterious Stranger and Other Cartoons* by John T. McCutcheon. It is in the public domain because its copyright has expired.

51. The painting of July from *Labors of the Month* by Simon
     Bening was created in the first half of the 16th century, and
     is in the public domain because its copyright has expired.
52. The illustration July by Hans Thoma is from his late 19th
     century book *Festkalendar.* It is in the public domain because
     its copyright has expired.

License Description and Terms

Aside from material purely in the public domain,
photographs and other material in this book are used
under specific licenses permitting free use, usually with
an attribution requirement. For full text and terms of these
licenses, click or enter the appropriate links below. If you
believe there is an error in the copyright status or
attribution of any of these images, please email us.

*   Creative Commons Attribution 2.0 Generic (CC-BY 2.0):
    http://creativecommons.org/licenses/by/2.0/deed.en
*   Creative Commons Attribution-Share Alike 3.0 Generic (CC-
    BY-SA 3.0): http://creativecommons.org/licenses/by-sa/
    3.0/
*   Creative Commons Attribution-Share Alike 2.5 Generic (CC-
    BY-SA 2.5): http://creativecommons.org/licenses/by-sa/
    2.5/deed.en
*   Creative Commons Attribution-Share Alike 2.0 Generic (CC-
    BY-SA 2.0): http://creativecommons.org/licenses/by/2.0/
    deed.en
*   Creative Commons Attribution-Share Alike 1.0 Generic (CC-
    BY-SA 1.0): http://creativecommons.org/licenses/by-sa/
    1.0/deed.en
*   CC0 1.0 Universal (CC0 1.0) Public Domain Dedication (CC0
    1.0) http://creativecommons.org/publicdomain/zero/1.0/
    deed.en
*   GNU Free Documentation License (GFDL): http://
    en.wikipedia.org/wiki/
    Wikipedia:Text_of_the_GNU_Free_Documentation_License
*   License Art Libre (Free Art License): http://artlibre.org

July, from the *Brevarium Grimani* by Simon Bening (c.1510)

Other Books from Timespinner Press

Timespinner
Press

The Story of a Special Day

Michael Dobson

A series of (eventually) 366 volumes covering everything that happened on your special day! Events, births, deaths, quotes, holidays, and much more. It's like a birthday card they'll never throw away!

US$7.95 print / US$2.99 ebook.

From Plassey to Pakistan

Humayun Mirza

The history of British Colonial India and the formation of Pakistan from the unique perspective of the son of Pakistan's first president and last of the royal line of Bengal, Bihar, and Orissa! This unique historical document tells the inside story of this distinguished family, including the detailed story of the coup that toppled his father from power!

US$27.95 print

A Whole New Navy: America's War in the Pacific

Miles Durr

The most comprehensive and detailed description of America's naval war in the Pacific ever—every battle, every ship, every task force and every task group from Pearl Harbor through the Japanese surrender! A must-have for the collection of every World War II buff!

US$29.95 print

Improbable History: The Weird, the Obscure, and the Strangely Important

edited by Michael Dobson

From the birth of Western civilization to the rescue of Apollo 13, from the Leaning Tower of Pisa to Florence's Duomo, history has often turned on small, improbable details. Whatever happened to the ancient Samaritan people? Why did a fortuitous rainstorm allow the British to conquer India? How did an air raid in Italy lead to the development of chemotherapy? What happened when Albert Einstein met Adolf Hitler on the streets of Berlin? How did the Japanese manage to attack the US mainland using balloons? A cast of award-winning writers tackle some of the strangest tales in history!

US$19.95 print

The Letters of William Philip Schwartz 1842-1855

edited by John F. Schwartz

The 19th century soldier and adventurer William Philip Schwartz wrote a series of vivid and detailed letters chronicling his adventures in the Indian Wars, the Mexican-American War, the Gold Rush, and his term as Marine sergeant aboard the USS Constellation. A pioneer in photography, he took *the first known war photographs*. An unforgettable first-hand look into life in the 19th century!

US$17.95 print

Watergate Considered as an Organization Chart of Semi-Precious Stones (and other essays)

by Michael Dobson

In this light-hearted yet insightful tour through the Nixon White House, the Committee to Re-Elect the President, and the various investigative committees, you'll meet fascinating characters from Richard Nixon himself to such lieutenants as a G. Gordon Liddy and John Dean. You'll gain insights into the origin of the scandal, the motives of the players, and how the situation spiraled so badly out of control.

US$9.95 print/US$3.99 ebook

July, by Hans Thoma

www.ingramcontent.com/pod-product-compliance
Lightning Source LLC
Chambersburg PA
CBHW060747260726
48660CB00002B/509